Flower Pot Pillow

MATERIALS:
12" pillow form • 4 buttons ½" • ½ yd satin ribbon ⅛" wide (Light Green, Ivory) • Needle and Thread • Fusible web • Stabilizer

FABRICS:
⅛ yd each Dark Lavender, Lavender print, Green print, Dark and Light Green solid • ⅔ yd Green-White stripe • 4½" x 4½" Peach print

Pot
Pattern
Cut 1

INSTRUCTIONS:
Make 22 Yo-Yos: Dark Lavender solid- 3 large flowers, 2 medium flowers, 2 medium buds • Lavender print- 3 medium for flowers, 2 medium for corners • Light Green print- 2 medium for wrapping buds, 2 medium for corners, 3 large Dark Green solid for folded leaves

Prep: Cut 2 squares of striped fabric 13" x 13".

Ruffle: Cut 2 strips of striped fabric 4" x 40". Sew strips end to end to make a 79½" long ruffle. Sew a ¼" hem along one edge. Sew a Gather stitch along the other edge. Pin and gather ruffle around one 13" square. Sew ruffle in place.

Flower Pot: Trace pattern for flower pot on fusible web and fuse to Peach fabric. Cut out. Fuse on pillow front. Pin stabilizer behind pot. Machine applique.

Buds: Fold 2 Dark Lavender medium Yo-Yos in half, stitch together for buds. Wrap each bud with a Light Green medium Yo-Yo, stitch to secure.

Leaves: Fold Dark Green large Yo-Yos in half. Stitch together for 6 leaves:

Flowers: Position flowers, leaves, and buds. Stitch in place. Sew buttons to centers. • Stitch 2 ribbon bow to corners.

Pillow: With right sides together, sew front to back ¼" inside ruffle stitching line. Leave a 9" opening for turning. Turn right side out.

Finish: Insert pillow form; stitch opening shut.

Denim & Lace Vest

MATERIALS:
Denim vest • 4" Ecru crocheted doily • 1½ yd Pale Green ⅜" wide satin ribbon • E-bead beads (Dark Mauve) • Light Green embroidery floss

FABRICS:
⅛ yd of Dark Mauve

INSTRUCTIONS:
Make Yo-Yos: Make 9 Mauve medium.

Doilies: Fold doily to form a basket for the flowers and sew to vest.

Yo-Yos: Create a bouquet above the basket doily by sewing 9 Mauve Yo-Yos in place. Sew beads in the center of each Yo-Yo.

Leaves: Cut 14 pieces of ribbon, each 3" long and fold to form narrow leaves. Sew leaves to bouquet.

Stems: Backstitch stems using 6 strands of floss.

Bow: Tie a bow with remaining ribbon and sew to top of basket.

Yo-Yo's and Fabric Flowers 3

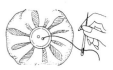

Yo-Yos with Buttons and Beads

Buttons. Buttons may be glued on with washable jewelry glue or sewn on using 2 strands of embroidery floss.

E Beads

Beads. Using a beading needle and thread, sew beads in place following the diagram above. Optional: Thread needle with 2 strands of embroidery floss.

Finished Quilt Assembly

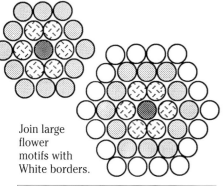

Join large flower motifs with White borders.

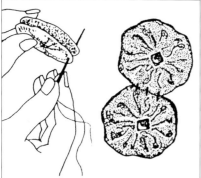

Attach Yo-Yos by placing the right side of two Yo-Yos together. Sew the edges with small whip stitches.

Flower Blossom Quilt

SIZE: 62" x 68"

FABRIC:

⅛ yd each (Dark Pink, Dark Yellow, Dark Green, Dark Blue)

⅝ yd each (Pink stripe, Light Green print, Light Blue print)

¾ yd Yellow check

1½ yd each (Dark Pink print, Dark Green print, Dark Blue print, Dark Yellow)

4 yds White solid

Make 907 large Yo-Yo's: 7 solids each (Dark Pink, Dark Green, Dark Blue) • 10 Dark Yellow solid • 42 each (Pink Stripe, Light Green print, Light Blue print) • 60 Yellow check • 84 each (Dark Pink print, Dark Green print, Dark Blue print) • 120 Dark Yellow print • 318 White solid.

Assembly: Following diagrams, make 7 motifs each of Pink, Green, and Blue and 10 motifs of Yellow. Stitch motifs together with White Yo-Yos.

Optional: Sew a ¾" button in the center Yo-Yo of each motif.

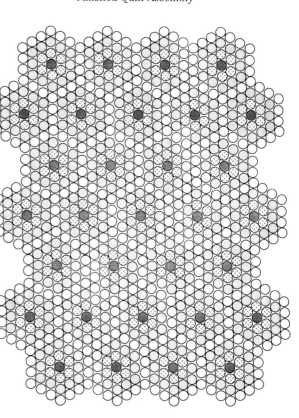

Log Cabin Quilt

INSTRUCTIONS:

All measurements include a 1/4" seam allowance.

Prep: Prewash fabric. Press.

A-B units: Cut 15 strips of fabrics A and B 1 1/2" x 40". With right sides together, sew A to B. Press. • Cut at 1 1/2" intervals to make 384 A-B units. Cut 48 B 1 1/2" squares.

Logs: Using various fabrics, cut 1 1/2" wide strips into 48 each of the following lengths:

Log 1: 1 1/2" • Log 2: 2 1/2" • Log 3: 3 1/2" • Log 4: 4 1/2" • Log 5: 5 1/2" • Log 6: 6 1/2" • Log 7: 7 1/2" • Log 8: 8 1/2"

Log Cabin Triangles: Join A-B units and logs in vertical rows following diagram. Sew B square to end of #8 log before sewing to log cabin.

Make 12 Blocks: Cut 12 White squares 12" x 12". Note: The A part of the A-B units will be sewn in half diagonally when attached to the block. Sew a Triangle to each corner. Press.

Assembly: Sew blocks together to form 4 rows. Press. • Sew rows together. Press.

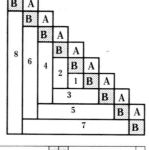

Borders: From fabric B, cut 8 inner border strips 2 1/2" x 40". Sew together end to end to make 300". Press. With right sides together, sew border to quilt. Press.
• From fabric C, cut 9 outer border strips 4 1/2" x 40". Sew together end to end to make 330". Press. With right sides together, sew border to quilt. Press.

Make 330 medium Yo-Yos: 208 Green, 122 Dark Red.

Flowers: Create flowers with Dark Red Yo-Yos. Stitch in place. Arrange Green Yo-Yos for leaves as shown in diagram. Sew to quilt. Sew bias tape in place for stems.

Quilting: Layer backing, batting and quilt top. Quilt as desired.

Binding: Cut 9 strips 2 1/2" x 40". Sew strips end to end to make 332". Press. Fold in half lengthwise. Press. • See Basic Instructions on page 18 to attach binding.

Finish: Sew Dark Red buttons on 3 flowers. • Sew buttons at block intersections as indicated on diagram.

Sew Logs

1. A / B + 1
2. A / B / 1 + A / B
3. A / B + 2 + A / B A / 1 B

SIZE: 72" x 92"

QUILT MATERIALS:
1 3/4 yds Cream for A • 3/4 yd Red for B • 1 yd Forest Green for C • 1/4 yd each 8 Dark small prints or solids • 76" x 96" backing and batting • 5/8 yd for binding • Green bias tape

YO-YO MATERIALS:
1/4 yd each (8 Green, 5 Dark Red) • Buttons (10 White 1", 45 Dark Red 1/2")

Sunflower Quilt

SIZE: 50" x 59"

QUILT MATERIALS:
$\frac{1}{2}$ yd Medium Blue
$\frac{1}{2}$ yd Blue print for C
$\frac{1}{2}$ yd Brown print for centers
$\frac{1}{4}$ yd Blue check
$2\frac{1}{4}$ yds White
$\frac{1}{2}$ yd Dark Green print
$\frac{1}{2}$ yd Dark Green solid
56" x 65" backing and batting
Blue embroidery floss
Optional: Fusible web

YO-YO MATERIALS:
$1\frac{5}{8}$ yds assorted Gold prints

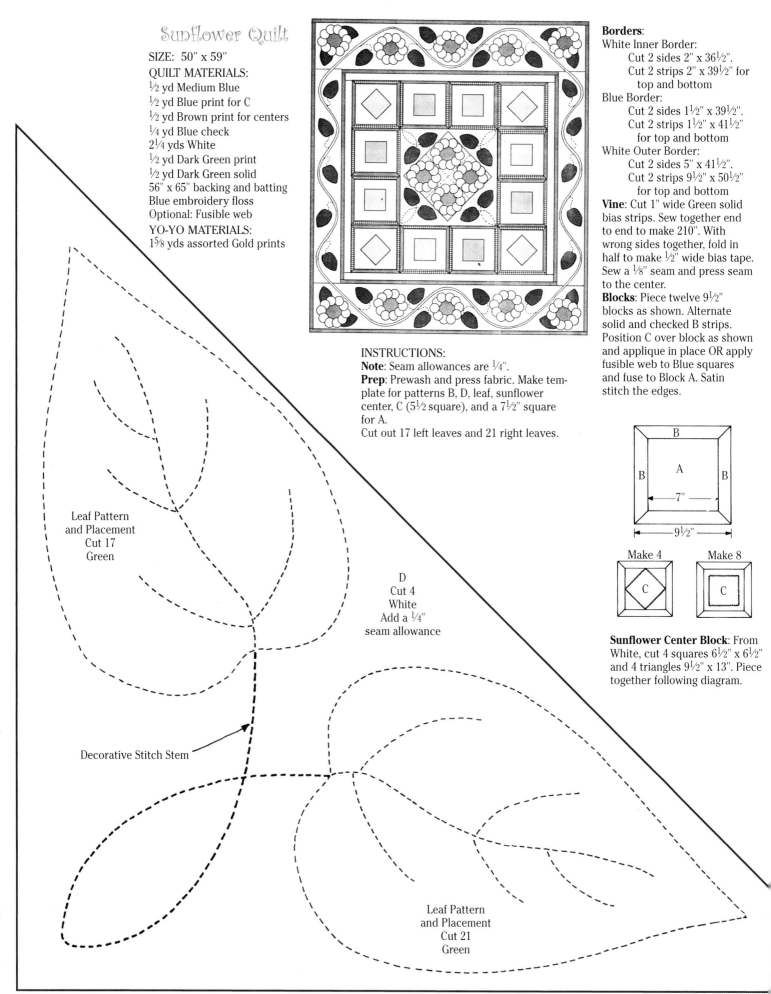

INSTRUCTIONS:
Note: Seam allowances are $\frac{1}{4}$".
Prep: Prewash and press fabric. Make template for patterns B, D, leaf, sunflower center, C ($5\frac{1}{2}$ square), and a $7\frac{1}{2}$" square for A.
Cut out 17 left leaves and 21 right leaves.

Borders:
White Inner Border:
    Cut 2 sides 2" x $36\frac{1}{2}$".
    Cut 2 strips 2" x $39\frac{1}{2}$" for top and bottom
Blue Border:
    Cut 2 sides $1\frac{1}{2}$" x $39\frac{1}{2}$".
    Cut 2 strips $1\frac{1}{2}$" x $41\frac{1}{2}$" for top and bottom
White Outer Border:
    Cut 2 sides 5" x $41\frac{1}{2}$".
    Cut 2 strips $9\frac{1}{2}$" x $50\frac{1}{2}$" for top and bottom
Vine: Cut 1" wide Green solid bias strips. Sew together end to end to make 210". With wrong sides together, fold in half to make $\frac{1}{2}$" wide bias tape. Sew a $\frac{1}{8}$" seam and press seam to the center.
Blocks: Piece twelve $9\frac{1}{2}$" blocks as shown. Alternate solid and checked B strips. Position C over block as shown and applique in place OR apply fusible web to Blue squares and fuse to Block A. Satin stitch the edges.

Sunflower Center Block: From White, cut 4 squares $6\frac{1}{2}$" x $6\frac{1}{2}$" and 4 triangles $9\frac{1}{2}$" x 13". Piece together following diagram.

Leaf Pattern and Placement Cut 17 Green

Decorative Stitch Stem

D
Cut 4
White
Add a $\frac{1}{4}$"
seam allowance

Leaf Pattern and Placement Cut 21 Green

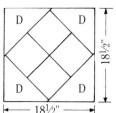

18½"

18½"

D D

D D

Machine applique a sunflower center in the middle of each square. Applique leaves and make veins and stems with the same size Satin stitch. Use a decorative stitch to make the stems. Join blocks as shown.

Assembly: Top and Bottom Rows: Alternate 9½" blocks. Sew together. Press.

Center: Sew two 9½" blocks together as shown in diagram. Press. Sew to the left side of the sunflower center block. Press. Sew two 9½" blocks together as shown in diagram. Press. Sew to the right side of the sunflower. Press. Sew the rows together. Press.

Borders:
Sew the White Inner border sides to the quilt. Press. Add the top and bottom borders. Press.
Sew the Blue sides to the quilt. Press. Add the top and bottom borders. Press.
Sew the White Outer border sides to the quilt. Press. Add the

top and bottom borders. Press.

Sunflowers: Machine applique sunflower centers across White top and bottom borders as shown. Applique leaves and create stems with the same size Satin stitch.

Vines: Place the seam of the bias strip against the quilt. Edge stitch the vine in place. Add leaves and stems.

Yo-Yos: Make 140 extra large Yo-Yos. Stitch 10 Yo-Yos in place for each sunflower.

Quick Turn Finish: With right sides together, layer backing and quilt top. Position batting over quilt top. Pin and sew around the edges leaving a 6" opening for turning. Turn the quilt right side out.
Stitch the opening shut. If desired, sew around the edge of the quilt. Quilt as desired.

Quilting Diagram

Cut on Fold

Sunflower Center
Cut 14
Dark Brown

To hand applique,
add ¼"
seam allowance

B
Cut 24 Blue Check
Cut 24 Medium Blue Solid
Add ¼"
seam allowance

Yo-Yo's and Fabric Flowers

Bad Hair Day Sweatshirt

MATERIALS:
Ivory sweatshirt • 6 assorted buttons • Permanet marking pens (Red, Black) • Blue washable fabric marker • Fusible web • Stabilizer

FABRICS:
½ yd Gold • 4½" x 7½" Peach • 3½" x 6" (Blue floral, Blue solid, 2 Blue prints)

INSTRUCTIONS:
Make 16 Yo-Yos: Gold- 4 large, 3 medium, 2 small • Blue solid- 3 medium • Blue prints- 2 each medium.

Prep: Cut 7 strips Gold fabric 1" x 9".

Appliques: Following manufacturer's instructions, trace patterns onto fusible web and fuse to fabrics. Pin appliques to shirt. Try shirt on to check placement. Fuse appliques in place. Draw facial features. Pin stabilizer behind appliques inside shirt. Machine applique all pieces. Remove stabilizer.

Yo-Yos: Cut a small slit across bottom center of medium and large Gold Yo-Yos. Position Yo-Yos around face for hair. Make a mark with washable marker through slit in Gold Yo-Yos. Remove Yo-Yos. Tack stitch center of each Gold strip on mark. Thread ends through slit in Yo-Yo and knot in place. Trim ends of strips at varying lengths. Stitch ends to shirt. Sew small Gold Yo-Yos in place for bangs. • Sew remaining Yo-Yos across bottom of blouse with 1 button in the center of each Yo-Yo.

Finish: Write words with a Blue washable marker. Go over the lines with a permanent Black pen.

Facial Details - We drew the face with a Blue wash-out marking pen following the design. Outline the details with a Black permanent marking pen. Use a Red pen for the mouth and cheeks.

I'M HAVING BAD HAIR DAY

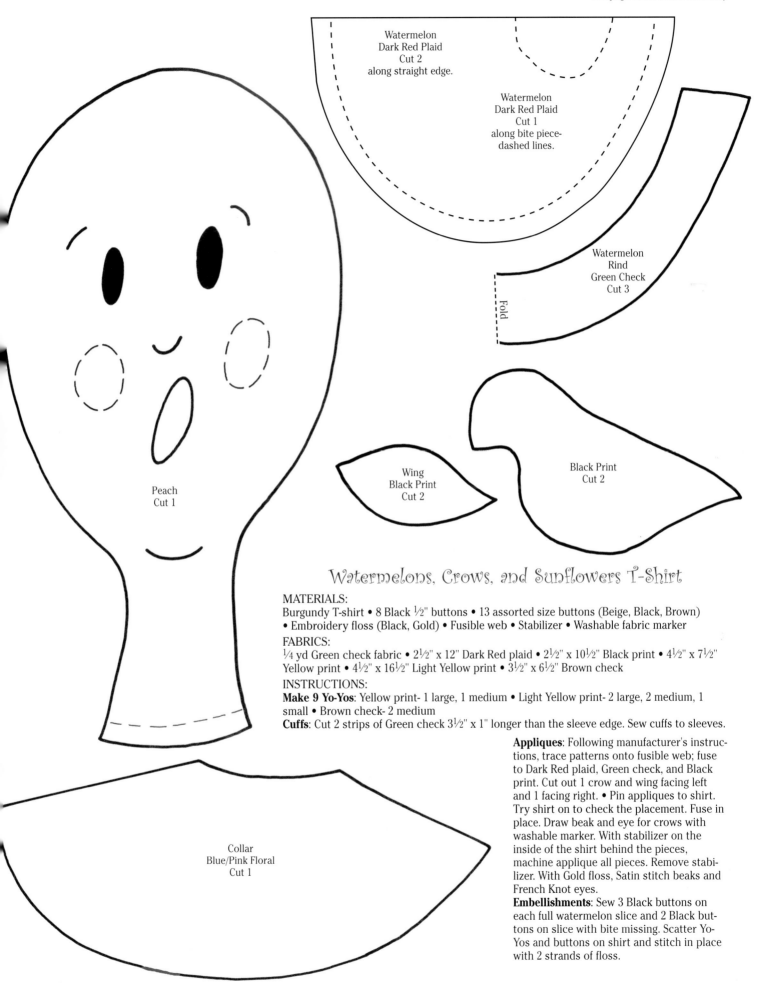

Watermelon
Dark Red Plaid
Cut 2
along straight edge.

Watermelon
Dark Red Plaid
Cut 1
along bite piece-
dashed lines.

Watermelon
Rind
Green Check
Cut 3

Fold

Peach
Cut 1

Wing
Black Print
Cut 2

Black Print
Cut 2

Collar
Blue/Pink Floral
Cut 1

Watermelons, Crows, and Sunflowers T-Shirt

MATERIALS:
Burgundy T-shirt • 8 Black ½" buttons • 13 assorted size buttons (Beige, Black, Brown)
• Embroidery floss (Black, Gold) • Fusible web • Stabilizer • Washable fabric marker

FABRICS:
¼ yd Green check fabric • 2½" x 12" Dark Red plaid • 2½" x 10½" Black print • 4½" x 7½"
Yellow print • 4½" x 16½" Light Yellow print • 3½" x 6½" Brown check

INSTRUCTIONS:
Make 9 Yo-Yos: Yellow print- 1 large, 1 medium • Light Yellow print- 2 large, 2 medium, 1
small • Brown check- 2 medium

Cuffs: Cut 2 strips of Green check 3½" x 1" longer than the sleeve edge. Sew cuffs to sleeves.

Appliques: Following manufacturer's instructions, trace patterns onto fusible web; fuse to Dark Red plaid, Green check, and Black print. Cut out 1 crow and wing facing left and 1 facing right. • Pin appliques to shirt. Try shirt on to check the placement. Fuse in place. Draw beak and eye for crows with washable marker. With stabilizer on the inside of the shirt behind the pieces, machine applique all pieces. Remove stabilizer. With Gold floss, Satin stitch beaks and French Knot eyes.

Embellishments: Sew 3 Black buttons on each full watermelon slice and 2 Black buttons on slice with bite missing. Scatter Yo-Yos and buttons on shirt and stitch in place with 2 strands of floss.

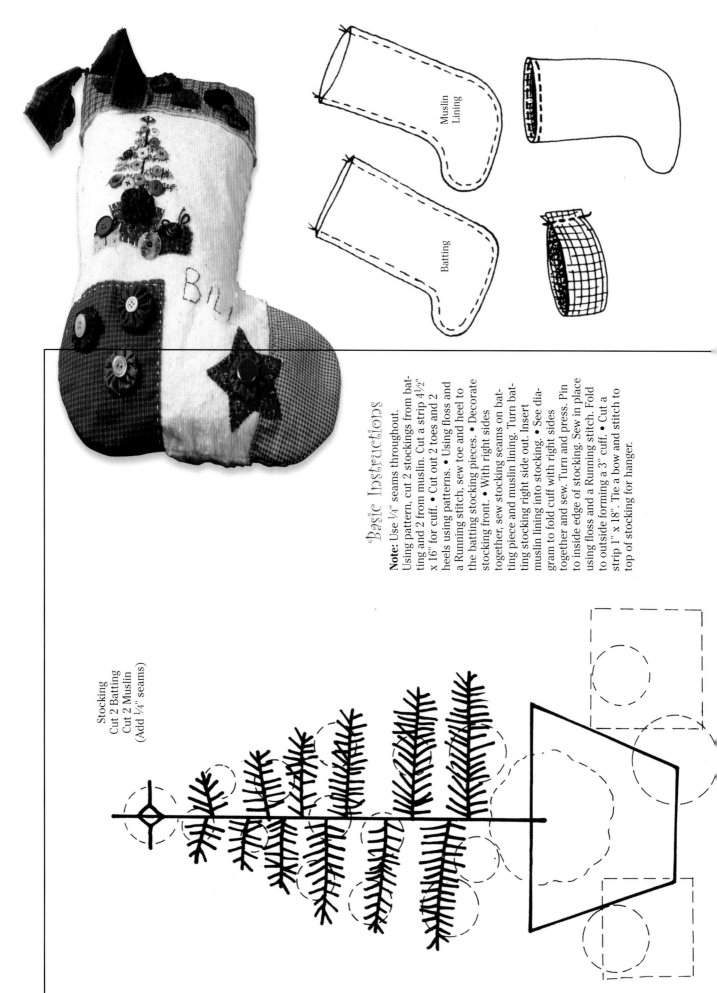

Muslin
Lining

Batting

Basic Instructions

Note: Use ¼" seams throughout.
Using pattern, cut 2 stockings from batting and 2 from muslin. Cut a strip 4½" x 16" for cuff. • Cut out 2 toes and 2 heels using patterns. • Using floss and a Running stitch, sew toe and heel to the batting stocking pieces. • Decorate stocking front. • With right sides together, sew stocking seams on batting piece and muslin lining. Turn batting stocking right side out. Insert muslin lining into stocking. • See diagram to fold cuff with right sides together and sew. Turn and press. Pin to inside edge of stocking. Sew in place using floss and a Running stitch. Fold to outside forming a 3" cuff. • Cut a strip 1" x 18". Tie a bow and stitch to top of stocking for hanger.

Stocking
Cut 2 Batting
Cut 2 Muslin
(Add ¼" seams)

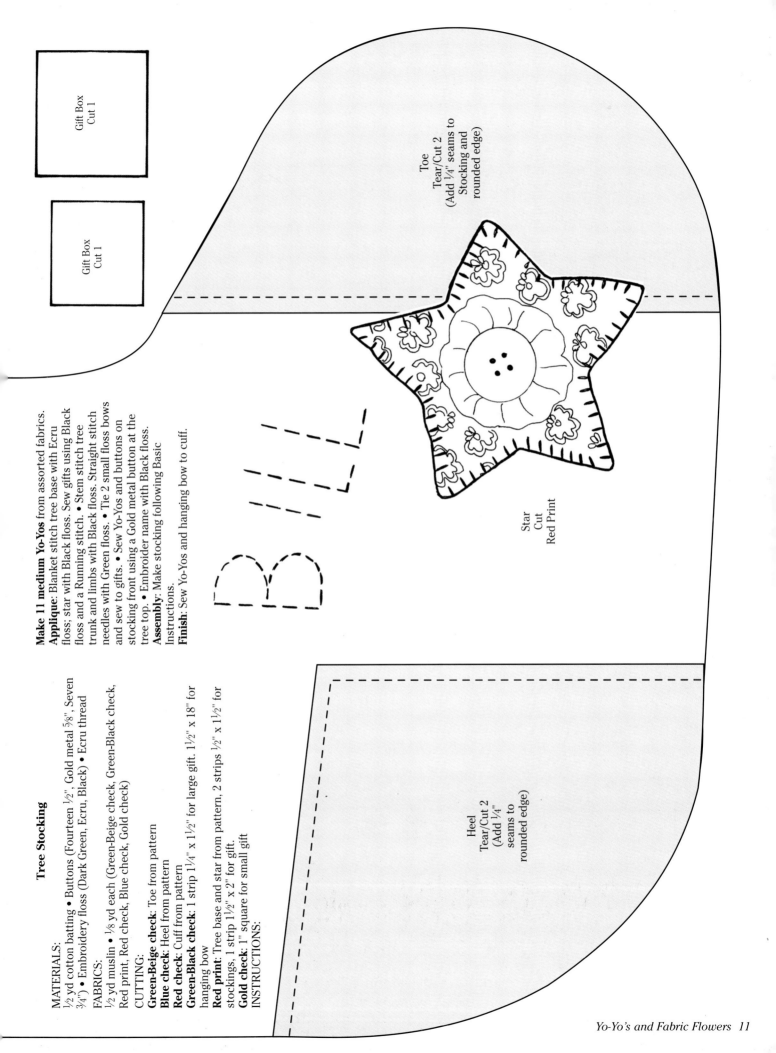

Tree Stocking

MATERIALS:
½ yd cotton batting • Buttons (Fourteen ½", Gold metal ⅝", Seven ¾") • Embroidery floss (Dark Green, Ecru, Black) • Ecru thread

FABRICS:
½ yd muslin • ⅛ yd each (Green-Beige check, Green-Black check, Red print, Red check, Blue check, Gold check)

CUTTING:
Green-Beige check: Toe from pattern
Blue check: Heel from pattern
Red check: Cuff from pattern
Green-Black check: 1 strip 1¼" x 1½" for large gift. 1½" x 18" for hanging bow
Red print: Tree base and star from pattern, 2 strips ½" x 1½" for stockings, 1 strip 1½" x 2" for gift.
Gold check: 1" square for small gift

INSTRUCTIONS:

Make 11 medium Yo-Yos from assorted fabrics.
Applique: Blanket stitch tree base with Ecru floss; star with Black floss. Sew gifts using Black floss and a Running stitch. • Stem stitch tree trunk and limbs with Black floss. Straight stitch needles with Green floss. • Tie 2 small floss bows and sew to gifts. • Sew Yo-Yos and buttons on stocking front using a Gold metal button at the tree top. • Embroider name with Black floss.
Assembly: Make stocking following Basic Instructions.
Finish: Sew Yo-Yos and hanging bow to cuff.

Gift Box
Cut 1

Gift Box
Cut 1

Toe
Tear/Cut 2
(Add ¼" seams to Stocking and rounded edge)

Star
Cut
Red Print

Heel
Tear/Cut 2
(Add ¼" seams to rounded edge)

Grapevine T-Shirt

MATERIALS:
Green T-shirt • Beads (Dark Green 6mm bugle, Green seed, Purple seed) • 1½ yds Dark Green satin ribbon ¼" wide • Dark Green embroidery floss

FABRICS:
⅛ yd each (2 Dark Green prints, 3 Purple prints)

INSTRUCTIONS:
Make 6 small Yo-Yos with each Purple print.
Prep: For each leaf, fold fabric right sides together and cut out. Sew all around the edge, slit the back and turn right side out. Make 2 leaves from 1 Green print and 2 leaves from other Green print. Press.
Left shoulder: Position leaf. Blanket stitch with 6 strands of floss. Sew Green bugle beads to make veins.
Right side: Position leaves. Stitch and bead as before. Position Yo-Yos, overlapping slightly to form bunch of grapes. Sew using 6 Purple seed beads in each center. Sew 4 Green 9mm bugle beads on leaves for veins.
Embroidery: Backstitch stems and tendrils.
Ribbon: Loop ribbons through and around grapes, up and over right shoulder, around neck, and join to leaf on left shoulder. Stitch in place using 2 Green beads every inch.

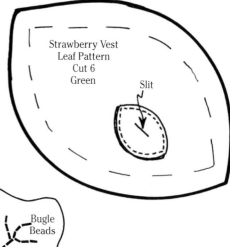

Strawberry Vest
Leaf Pattern
Cut 6
Green

Slit

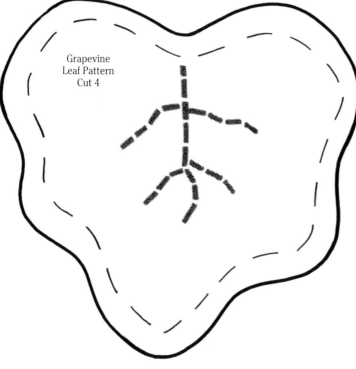

Grapevine
Leaf Pattern
Cut 4

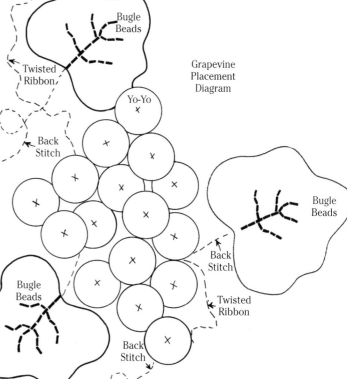

Bugle Beads

Twisted Ribbon

Back Stitch

Yo-Yo

Grapevine Placement Diagram

Bugle Beads

Back Stitch

Twisted Ribbon

Bugle Beads

Back Stitch

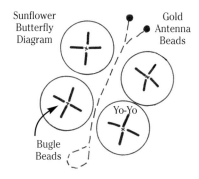

Sunflower Butterfly Diagram

Gold Antenna Beads

Yo-Yo

Bugle Beads

Sunflower T-Shirt

MATERIALS:
Yellow T-shirt • E-beads (Gold, Dark Green iridescent) • 9mm bugle beads (Gold, Green, Red) • Seed beads (Dark Green, Red) • 2 Gold 4mm beads • 10" Green satin ¼" wide ribbon • 7" Black satin rattail cord

FABRICS:
⅛ yd each (4 Gold prints, 1 Black print, 2 Green prints) • 6½" x 6½" Red print

INSTRUCTIONS:
Make 49 small Yo-Yos: 30 assorted Gold, 10 assorted Green, 7 Black print, 2 Red print.

Flower center: Pin Black Yo-Yos on shirt front, overlapping edges slightly. Sew using 3 iridescent e-bead beads in each center. Sew edges to shirt.

Petals: Pin 28 Gold Yo-Yos around the center. Sew using 1 Gold E-bead and 4 Gold bugle beads. Sew edges to shirt.

Leaves and stem: Pin 10 Green Yo-Yos 3" below flower for leaves. Sew using 4 Green bugle beads. Sew edges to shirt.

Ribbon: Pin ribbon as shown in photo. Twist ribbon. Stitch in place using 3 Green seed beads every inch.

Butterfly: Using 2 Gold and 2 Red Yo-Yos, form butterfly following diagram. Sew with 4 Red bugle beads. Sew edges to shirt. Fold Black rattail cord in half and twist. Sew in place using 3 Red seed beads at each stitch. Sew a Gold 4mm beads on ends of cord for antennae.

Yo-Yo's

Sunflower T-Shirt Placement Diagram

Twisted Ribbon

Leaf Yo-Yo's

Top

Bugle Beads

Button

Yo-Yo

Bugle Beads

Back Stitch

Leaf

Back Stitch

Twisted/ Ribbon

Strawberry Vest

MATERIALS:
Ecru vest • 8 Green ½" buttons • 3 yd Dark Green ribbon ⅛" wide • Beads (Red E-bead, Green seed, Red 9mm bugle, Red 15mm bugle, Green 9mm bugle) • Green embroidery floss

FABRICS:
⅛ yd each (1 Green print, 3 Red prints)

INSTRUCTIONS:
Make 8 small Red Yo-Yos for strawberry vine.

Left side: For each pattern, fold fabric right sides together. Cut out. Sew all around the edge. Slit the back and clip curves. Turn right side out. Press. Make 6 Green leaves for strawberry cluster.

• Position leaves on left side of vest. Blanket stitch with 6 strands of floss.

• Position berries and sew in place using a Red E-bead. • See diagram to loop ribbons for vines and tendrils. Sew in place using 3 Green seed beads on each stitch. See diagram to Backstitch berry stems with 6 strands of Green floss. • See diagram for button placement and sew 8 Green buttons to tops of Yo-Yos.

• Sew groups of two 9mm and one 15mm Red bugle beads to tendrils. Sew 4 Green 9mm bugle beads on leaves for veins.

Yo-Yo's and Fabric Flowers 13

Sunflower Sweatshirt

MATERIALS:
Black sweatshirt with set in sleeves • 3 White crocheted 4" doilies • Rit Gold dye • Buttons (11 Red ⅝", 8 Dark Green ⅝", 9 Black ⅜", 9 Red ⅜", 4 Black ¼" ball) • 3 small Gold beads • Embroidery floss (Gold, Dark Red) • Fusible web • Stabilizer

FABRICS:
⅛ yd each (Dark Red print, Gold print, Dark Green print, Dark Blue, Bright Green print, Black-Brown print, Red dot print)

INSTRUCTIONS:
Dye doilies Gold following manufacturer's instructions. Let dry.

Make 7 Yo-Yos: Black-Brown- 3 medium for doilies, 3 small for bird wings • Red dot- 1 small for ladybug.

Patchwork squares: Cut 3 each 3¼ x 3¼ squares from Dark Red, Dark Green, and Gold. Following manufacturer's instructions, apply web to squares. Position squares on shirt ½" apart. Fuse in place. Pin stabilizer inside shirt behind squares. Machine applique squares. • Gather doilies in center and stitch to Dark Red squares. Sew large Brown Yo-Yos to centers of doilies with a Red button.

Appliques: Following manufacturer's instructions, trace patterns onto web, cut out, and fuse to fabrics for birds, watermelons, and ladybug. Fuse birds to Gold squares, watermelons and ladybug to Dark Green squares. Pin stabilizer behind shapes and machine applique. Sew Red dot Yo-Yo to ladybug with small Red button and sew 4 ball buttons around the Yo-Yo. • Sew small Black-Brown Yo-Yos to bird wings with a Black button. Sew a Gold bead for bird eye. Satin stitch the beak and Stem stitch the legs with 6 strands of Dark Red floss. • Sew 3 Black buttons to each watermelon for seeds. • Sew large Red and Green buttons to corners of squares.

Shirt: Cut off sleeves and ribbing on neck and bottom of shirt. Fold raw edges under ⅜" and Blanket stitch with 6 strands of Gold floss.

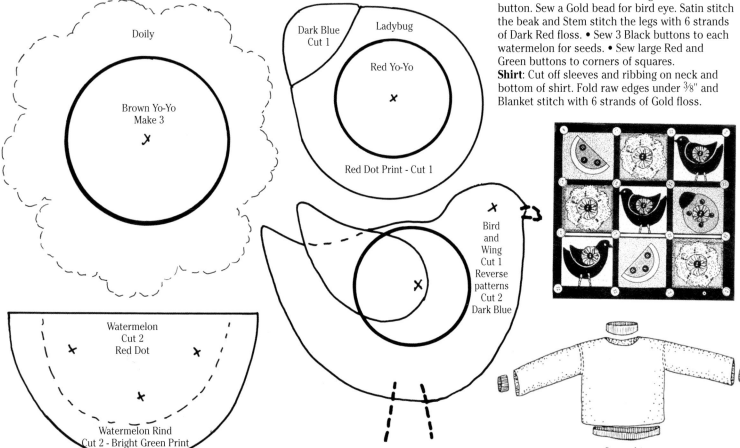

Doily

Brown Yo-Yo
Make 3

Dark Blue
Cut 1

Ladybug

Red Yo-Yo

Red Dot Print - Cut 1

Bird and Wing
Cut 1
Reverse patterns
Cut 2
Dark Blue

Watermelon
Cut 2
Red Dot

Watermelon Rind
Cut 2 - Bright Green Print

Sweatshirt
Cut off sleeves and ribbing on neck and bottom of shirt.

Stitch Directory

Running Stitch - Come up at A. Weave the needle through the fabric, making short, even stitches.

Tack Stitch - Bring needle up through garment, take a small stitch, then go down.

Backstitch - Come up at A, go down at B. Come back up at C. Repeat.

Stem Stitch - Using 6 strands of embroidery floss, backstitch stems.

Whip Stitch - Work from left to right to make regular, slanting stitches along the stitch line. Bring the needle up above the center of the previous stitch.

Chain Stitch - Come up at A. To form a loop, hold the thread down with your thumb, go down at B (as close as possible to A). Come back up at C with the needle tip over the thread. Repeat to form a chain.

Lazy Daisy Stitch - Come up at A. Go down at B (right next to A) to form a loop. Come back up at C with needle tip over thread. Go down at D to make a small anchor stitch over top of loop.

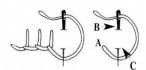

Blanket Stitch - Come up at A, hold the thread down with your thumb, go down at B. Come back up at C with the needle tip over the thread. Pull the stitch into place. Repeat, outlining with the bottom legs of the stitch. Use this stitch to edge fabrics.

Feather Stitch - Bring needle from back of fabric into the fold. Poke the needle back down through background fabric right next to the place where you came out. Pull gently, avoiding puckers. Push the needle back into the fold for about 1/8". Pull the thread through and insert needle into background fabric, keeping the thread at right angles to the fold.

Satin Stitch for Flower Stems - Work small straight stitches close together and at the same angle to fill an area with stitches. Vary the length of the stitches as required to keep the outline of the area smooth.

Beaded Ribbon - Bring needle from back of fabric through the ribbon, string 3 beads, pass needle down through ribbon. Twist ribbon and repeat.

Applique or Blind Stitch - (Slip Stitch) Bring needle and thread through folded edge of applique. Pick up a thread or two from the background fabric. Insert needle back through edge. Continue around applique.

Hearts and Stars T-Shirt

MATERIALS:
Red T-shirt • 3 White crocheted 4" doilies • Buttons (7 Yellow 1/2", 2 Red 1/2", 6 Red 3/8", 16 Red 1") • Fusible web • Stabilizer • Rit Gold fabric dye

FABRICS:
1/4 yd of each (Blue-Black stripe, Blue-Black dot, Blue-Black check, Gold, Red, Gold print, Red print)

INSTRUCTIONS:
Dye doilies Gold following manufacturer's instructions. Let dry.

Make 12 Yo-Yos: Gold print- 3 medium, 3 small • Gold- 1 small • Red- 5 small.

Patchwork squares: Cut 3 each 3 1/4" x 3 1/4" squares from Blue-Black stripe, Blue-Black dot, and Blue-Black check. Following manufacturer's instructions, apply web to squares. Position squares on shirt 1/2" apart. Fuse in place. Pin stabilizer inside shirt behind squares. Machine applique squares. • Gather doilies in center and stitch to Blue-Black dot squares. Center a medium Gold print Yo-Yo on each doily. Place a small Red Yo-Yo on top. Stitch to shirt with a Yellow button.

Appliques: Following manufacturer's instructions, trace patterns onto web, cut out, and fuse to fabrics for 3 stars, 2 hearts, and moon. Fuse stars to striped squares, hearts and moon to check squares. Pin stabilizer behind shapes and machine applique. Sew small Gold print Yo-Yos to star squares with a Yellow button. Sew small Gold print Yo-Yo above moon with a Yellow button. • Sew Red Yo-Yos on hearts. Sew 3 small Red buttons below Yo-Yos on hearts. • Sew large Red buttons to corners of squares.

Gather doilies in center.

Black and White Vest

MATERIALS:
½ yd each of 6 prints (Black, White) • 202 buttons ½" to ¾"

INSTRUCTIONS:
Make 202 large Yo-Yos. • Refer to diagram. Sew Yo-Yos together. Sew together at 2 sides and top points. Leave a slit on each side of vest by not stitching the Yo-Yos on Rows 1 and 2. • Sew shoulder Yo-Yos. • Sew a button to each Yo-Yo.

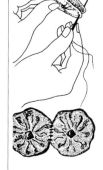

Attach yo–yos by placing the right side of two yo-yos together. Sew the edges with small whip stitches.

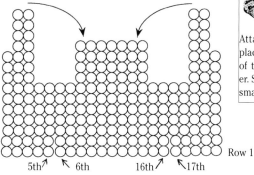

Row 1

5th↑ ↖ 6th   16th↑ ↖ 17th

Do not stitch between 5th & 6th and 16th & 17th Yo-Yos on Rows 1 and 2.

White Vest

MATERIALS:
36 Maroon buttons ¾" • 9mm bugle beads (Pink, Green) • E beads (Pink, Green)
FABRICS:
4¼ yds White • 1⅝ yds Green
INSTRUCTIONS:
Make 512 medium Yo-Yos (160 Moss Green, 352 White) Start on Row 6. Referring to diagram, stitch Yo-Yos together. • Sew shoulders together. Sew Green Yo-Yos around the edge of vest and sleeves. Sew buttons on White Yo-Yos around 2 edge front rows and neck row.

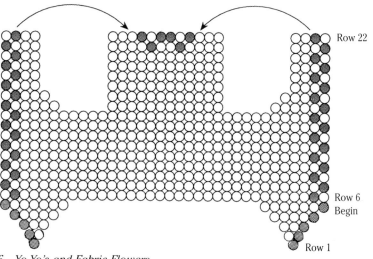

Row 22

Row 6
Begin

Row 1

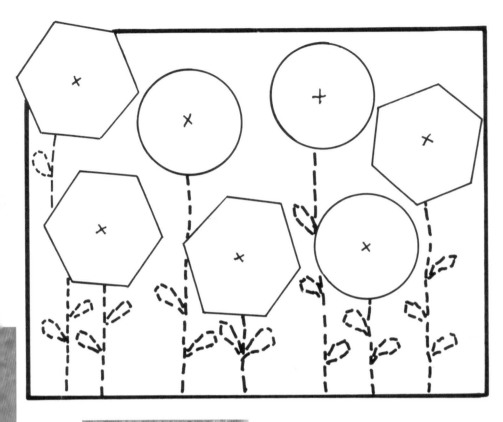

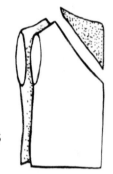

Sweatshirt Vest

MATERIALS:
Black sweatshirt with set-in sleeves • Buttons (15 Red, 9 Green, 3 large Yellow, 2 small Yellow, 3 Brown, 2 Blue) • Embroidery floss (Red, Gold, Blue, Green)

FABRICS:
1/8 yd each (Gold print, Green print, Blue print, Red print)

INSTRUCTIONS:
Make 34 Yo-Yos: Blue- 3 large, 2 medium • Red- 15 small • Gold- 2 small, 3 medium • Green- 2 small, 7 medium.

Vest: Cut bottom and neck ribbing off shirt. Cut off sleeves at shoulder seam. Fold shirt in half and cut center front in a V shape. • Blanket stitch armholes with 6 strands of Gold floss on the left and Blue floss on the right. Blanket stitch front edge with Red floss.

Pockets: Using sleeve fabric, cut 2 pockets 6 1/2" x 7 1/2". Fold raw edges under 1/2", pin 2" from bottom and 3" from the center edge. Blanket stitch in place using 6 strands of Green floss on left pocket, Gold floss on right pocket.

Finish: Stitch Yo-Yos in place with buttons. Stem stitch flower stems with 6 strands of Green floss.

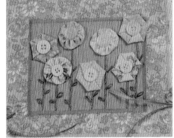

Flower Garden Patch

MATERIALS:
7 Yellow 1/2" Buttons • Green embroidery floss • Fusible web • Stabilizer

FABRICS:
1/4 yd each (Blue-Pink-Yellow print, Yellow-Blue print) • 1/8 yd each (Pink print, Pink check, Blue stripe, Blue-Yellow print)

INSTRUCTIONS:
Make 7 small Yo-Yos: Pink check- 1 folded • Pink print- 1 folded, 1 open • Blue print- 1 open • Yellow print- 2 open, 1 folded.

Frames: Cut Blue-Pink-Yellow print 6" x 7" for outer frame. Cut Blue stripe 4" x 5" for center. Following manufacturer's instructions, apply fusible web to all fabrics.

Finish: Position Blue stripe. Fuse fabrics in place. Pin stabilizer behind pieces and machine applique. • Position Yo-Yos and sew a 1/2" button in the center. • With 6 strands of Green floss, Stem stitch stems and make Lazy Daisy leaves.

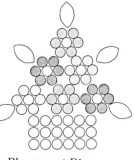

Placement Diagram
for Back of Vest

Large Leaf
Cut 10

enlarge
patterns
200%

Small Leaf
Cut 12

Flowers Vest

MATERIALS:
Dark Green sweatshirt • 1 skein each embroidery floss (Teal, Light Green, Dark Green) • 26 Antique metal buttons

FABRICS:
1 yd Teal fabric • ½ yd Dark Green for Yo-Yos • ½ yd Green floral for leaves • ½ yd Pink print for flower • ¼ yd Yellow for flower centers, • large Yo-Yo • ¼ yd Yellow floral for 3 flower centers • ¼ yd Light Pink print for flower • ¼ yd Mauve print for flower • ¼ yd Blue print for flower • ¼ yd Light Green print for flower • ¼ yd Dark Pink for large Yo-Yo flower

INSTRUCTIONS:
Vest: Make sweatshirt into vest. Blanket stitch edges with Teal floss.
Make Yo-Yos: Teal- 26 small • Dark Green- 10 small • 6 small from all 6 flower fabrics for bouquet • Yellow- 3 small for bouquet centers, 1 large for front • Yellow floral-3 small for bouquet centers • Dark Pink- 1 large for front
Neckline: Sew 10 Dark Green and 8 Teal Yo-Yos around neck edge starting at the center back, alternating colors.
Basket: Make 3 rows with 6 Teal Yo-Yos in each row. Whipstitch Yo-Yos together; tack to center bottom of back.
Make 6 Flowers for Basket: Row 1: 2 floral Yo-Yos. • Row 2: 1 floral, 1 Yellow center, 1 floral. • Row 3: 2 floral. • Sew button to center Yo-Yo. Make 6 flowers. Place 3 flowers above basket, tack to vest. Add second row of 2 flowers and a top row with remaining flower. Sew bow charm on basket.
Front: Sew Teal Yo-Yos and buttons to center of both large Yo-Yos.

Tack large flowers to left and right side of center front.
Leaves: Make patterns for leaves. Fold each leaf fabric right sides together. Cut out 5 large and 6 small leaves. Sew all around the edge of each leaf. Slit the back and turn right side out. • Using Green floss, Blanket stitch 5 large leaves to flowers in basket, 2 small leaves to each large flower on the front, and 2 small leaves to flowers on the neck. Backstitch veins and tendrils with 3 strands of Light Green floss.

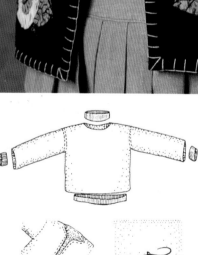

Make Fabric Binding: Cut 3" wide strips of fabric on the bias. Sew end to end to make 3 yards of bias tape. Fold in half lengthwise and press. Fold each edge to center fold line and press again. Cut bias tape to length needed plus 1".

Basic Materials:
Sweatshirts, Buttons, Charms • Cotton fabric • Needle, Sewing thread, Embroidery floss

Sweatshirt: Use a set-in sleeve sweatshirt 1 size larger than normal. Remove neck band, cuffs and bottom band by cutting in the ditch. For vests, cut off sleeves.

Even Edges: Measure from underarms to desired length plus ¾". Cut off. Fold shirt in half, cut the center.
Turn under ¾" and machine stitch close to raw edge. Repeat with another row of stitching.
Attach Fabric Binding:
Sew binding to jacket with a ½" seam. Fold tape to wrong side of garment Stitch to shirt.

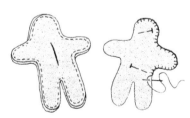

Appliques: Fold fabric with right sides together. Cut out applique using both layers. With right sides together, sew around the shape. Clip curves and trim seams. Make a small slit in 1 layer of fabric. Turn right side out. Press. Pin to garment. Blind stitch or Blanket stitch in place.